T0347435

Alice

IN HER OWN WORDS

Also available:
Rule Britannia: an anthology of patriotic poems
War Poets: an anthology
William Wordsworth Anthology
William Shakespeare Sonnets
William Shakespeare Quotations

Written by Annie Bullen.
The author has asserted her moral rights.
Edited by Abbie Wood.
Designed by Jemma Cox.

Available through mail order. See our website,
www.thehistorypress.co.uk, for our full range of titles,
or contact us for a copy of our brochure.

Pitkin Publishing, The History Press, The Mill,
Brimscombe Port, Stroud, Gloucestershire, GL5 2QG.
Sales and enquiries: 01453 883300
Email: sales@thehistorypress.co.uk

Printed in India
ISBN: 978-1-84165-377-8   1/15

CONTENTS

The Young Don   4

White Stone Days – Wonderland is Born   12

Alice's Oxford   19

Mean What You Say!   27

Conversations with Curious Creatures   36

We're All Mad Here   44

Of Cabbages and Kings   52

Off With Their Heads!   63

You're Nothing But a Pack of Cards!   72

THE YOUNG DON

⚬⚬⚬

The two-storey parsonage was
roomy and a wonderful home for
a large family of children, despite
its isolation in the Cheshire
countryside. Two girls were born
first and then, in 1892, a boy,
christened at his father's church,
All Saints', in Daresbury, with
the names Charles Lutwidge (his
mother's maiden name) Dodgson.
More children arrived – eleven in
all: seven girls and four boys. It fell
to Charles, the eldest son, to look
after and lead the others in games,
expeditions and entertainments.
In those days of self-sufficiency, he
would write poetry and puzzles,
build tiny tool kits and puppet

theatres, design magazines and newsletters for family enjoyment, invent games, and put to use home and garden implements to keep his siblings – especially his sisters – amused. It was important to him to be the acknowledged head of this little band, whom he called 'the children of the north'.

Charles Dodgson's lifelong pleasure in the company of young children stemmed from those days, first in Daresbury and, later, when he was 11, at Croft in Yorkshire, his father's next parish.

Preserved copies of *The Rectory Umbrella*, one of the 'publications' he produced for family entertainment, are an early indication of the fantasy and the poetry that were to run through all his later works for his young friends. The frontispiece shows a cheerful bearded man, reclining on the ground under the shade of a large umbrella on whose panels are written: 'jokes', 'riddles', 'fun', 'poetry' and 'tales'. He is attended by fairy figures representing good humour, mirth, content, knowledge and liveliness, while the stormy boulders hurled from the sky by malicious sprites of woe and spite are deflected by the large umbrella. The 'umbrella tree', an ancient yew which still stands in the grounds of Croft Rectory, was the inspiration for the title of the magazine. The four lines of verse written by the young Charles foreshadow his famous later rhymes: *All day he sat without a hat, That comical old feller, Shading his form from the driving storm, With the Rectory Umbrella.*

This talented child was born into a happy and industrious family. His parents, Charles and Fanny (Frances Jane), were cousins; she was sweet-natured and patient, he clever and conscientious. There were servants in the rectory, but many of the chores fell on the shoulders of Fanny and her children. Until the young Charles was 12 years old, he and his brothers and sisters were taught at home by both their parents.

Charles Dodgson senior, the parson, was a gifted mathematician who had won a double first at Christ Church Oxford. He took in pupils to supplement his income and nurtured high hopes for his eldest son who, along with his talent to amuse and entertain, had inherited his father's mathematical ability.

So Charles junior was sent to boarding school at nearby Richmond for 18 months and then endured rather than enjoyed more than three years at Rugby, where he won many academic prizes but proved to be poor at games.

When he went up to Oxford in 1851 he did so with the memory of Rugby behind him, but carrying always the appetite for learning inculcated by his parents and the 'safety blanket' of his large and happy family. Charles Lutwidge Dodgson, a tall, thin young man, a little shy and with a stammer, and deaf in one ear from a childhood illness, was leaving one small secure environment for another – just as enclosed but with greater opportunities. Christ Church College (known in Oxford as *Aedes Christi* or

The House) was to be his home for the rest of his life.

By this time he was a meticulous letter-writer, obsessive about keeping the many gadgets in his rooms in order, and later he was methodical about recording his observations in his diary. He won first-class honours in mathematics and was awarded a second in classical moderations, becoming a 'student' (the Christ Church equivalent of a Fellowship) at his college, a mathematics don and sub-librarian of Christ Church.

Maths was his subject, but he longed to break into the literary world, writing poetry, prose, puzzles and essays for newspapers. In case of publication, he needed a pen-name and, with his penchant for brainteasers, would not settle for a name plucked from the air.

He translated his name Charles Lutwidge loosely into Latin: Carolus Ludovicus (Lewis); he then transposed and anglicised the names to Lewis Carroll.

In 1956 he discovered a new passion – photography. By the time he moved into a new set of rooms in the north-west corner of The House's Tom Quad, he was given permission to build a glass photographic studio on the roof – and the freedom to photograph many celebrities of the day, including Poet Laureate Alfred Tennyson, members of the Millais family, and Frederick, the Crown Prince of Denmark. But his favourite subjects were young children, especially small girls who reminded him of his sisters and for whom he made up stories and nonsense rhymes and kept a dressing-up box of costumes to wear when they were in front of the camera.

Wonderland was born in 1855 when Henry George Liddell, the new Dean, arrived at Christ Church with his family, including the three-year-old Alice who was to become the great inspiration for the genius of the child-doting don.

WHITE STONE DAYS
– WONDERLAND IS BORN

All in the golden afternoon
Full leisurely we glide;
For both our oars, with little skill,
By little arms are plied,
While little hands make vain pretence
Our wanderings to guide.

That 'golden afternoon' saw the
conception of *Alice's Adventures
in Wonderland*. The rhyme refers
to a boating expedition made in
early July 1862 when Dodgson
and his friend Reverend Robinson
Duckworth took the three young
Liddell sisters – Lorina, Alice and
Edith – in a rowing boat on the

Thames upstream from Folly Bridge to Godstowe.

Dodgson was punctilious in keeping his diary; he had the curious habit of marking special days with the mention of the words 'white stone'. This day was a definite 'white stone' occasion.

The first special day of this sort concerning the Liddell children was marked a few years earlier, in 1856, when Alice's father became Dean of Christ Church. Alice and her two sisters were playing in the Deanery garden when Dodgson turned up with his camera to photograph the cathedral. The little girls rushed up to him, clamouring for their pictures to be taken. Dodgson and the children became firm friends and days were spent enjoying boating picnics on the river and expeditions in and around Oxford, where stories would be told, songs sung, photographs taken, and riddles and word games played.

But the 'golden afternoon' had a momentum all of its own.

As Dodgson and Duckworth rowed, the children sculled for short stretches, but were soon begging for stories. Without planning what he was going to say, Dodgson sent his protagonist, Alice, on a dream journey down the rabbit-hole and into a land peopled with extraordinary creatures and strange characters.

'It was much pleasanter at home,' thought poor Alice, 'when one wasn't always growing larger and smaller, and being ordered around by mice and

*rabbits. I almost wish I hadn't gone down
that rabbit-hole – and yet – and yet – it's
rather curious, you know, this sort of life!
I do wonder what **can** have happened
to me! When I used to read fairy-tales,
I fancied that kind of thing never
happened, and now here I am in the
middle of one! There ought to be a book
written about me, that there ought! …'*

The storybook Alice, wedged in the
White Rabbit's tiny house, ponders
thus as she grows too large to escape.
Dodgson took these words from the
real Alice who, on their return to
the Deanery, begged her friend to
write out 'Alice's adventures'. Later,
Robinson Duckworth would say that
Dodgson worked through the night,
writing down what he remembered.
Two years later, for Christmas 1864,
this perfectionist presented Alice

with a manuscript copy of 'Alice's Adventures Under Ground'.

He admitted in his introductory poem to the book that every time his storytelling flagged on that summer's day, he was implored by the three girls to carry on. Despite growing weariness and the fear of running out of ideas, he did so. Although he said his stories normally 'lived and died like summer midges', this time it was to be different:

Ah cruel Three! In such an hour,
Beneath such dreamy weather,
To beg a tale of breath too weak
To stir the tiniest feather!
Yet what can one poor voice avail
Against three tongues together?

Thus grew the tale of Wonderland:
Thus slowly, one by one,

Its quaint events were hammered out –
And now the tale is done,
And home we steer, a merry crew
Beneath the setting sun.

Alice's sisters, Lorina and Edith, play their parts in the story as the Lory and the Eaglet in the pool of tears. Duckworth is the Duck and Dodgson the Dodo, who is chided for his pomposity: *'Speak English!' said the Eaglet. 'I don't know the meaning of half of those long words, and, what's more, I don't believe you do either!'* But it is Alice, who was ten at the time (although the Alice in the story is only seven), who is the heroine and for whom the book that has enthralled children ever since was written.

Later, Dodgson, still inspired by Alice, was to send her into the land behind the Looking-Glass. But she was growing up and he knew that his child-friend would soon be entering adulthood and growing away from him. He portrays himself as the bumbling White Knight who rescues her from the clutches of the Red Knight, and helps her in her bid to become a Queen by escorting her across the brook which symbolises the divide between childhood and adolescence:

'You've only a few yards to go,' he said, 'down the hill and over that little brook, and then you'll be a Queen – But you'll stay and see me off first?' he added as Alice turned with an eager look in the direction to which he pointed. 'I shan't be long. You'll wait and wave your handkerchief when I get to that turn in the road? I think it'll encourage me, you see.'

ALICE'S OXFORD

Many of the observations and characters that run through the pages of *Alice's Adventures in Wonderland* refer to people, customs and objects to be found in Oxford.

'Once upon a time there were three little sisters,' the Dormouse began in a great hurry; 'and their names were Elsie, Lacie and Tillie; and they lived at the bottom of a well –'
'What did they live on?' said Alice, who always took a great interest in questions of eating and drinking.
'They lived on treacle,' said the Dormouse, after thinking a minute or two.

'They couldn't have done that, you know,' Alice gently remarked; *'they'd have been ill.'*
'So they were,' said the Dormouse; *'very ill.'*

Alice's father was Dean of Christ Church, the cathedral built on the shrine of St Frideswide, Oxford's patron saint, whose holy well was at nearby Binsey. Today you can see the saint's shrine in the cathedral, close to the beautiful Edward Burne-Jones window depicting her story. Alice often walked along the towpath to Binsey with her sisters and governess, Miss Prickett ('Pricks'), and knew about the 'treacle' well, so-called from medieval times when the word 'treacle' denoted a healing fluid. The well and its healing water are said to have miraculously

appeared in answer to the saintly
Frideswide's prayers when her
unwanted suitor and pursuer, King
Algar, was struck blind. He was
healed and she built her priory on
the spot.

The three little girls, Elsie, Lacie
and Tillie, were the young Liddells:
Lorina Charlotte (LC), Alice (an
anagram of Lacie) and Edith (whose
nickname was Tillie).

'Found what?' said the Duck.
'Found it,' the Mouse replied rather
crossly: 'of course you know what "it"
means.'
'I know what "it" means well enough,
when I find a thing,' said the Duck: 'it's
generally a frog or a worm …'

Alice and her sisters were often
taken on boating expeditions by

Charles Dodgson (as the Dodo in Wonderland he organises the Caucus-race) and one of his friends. Reverend Robinson Duckworth (later Canon of Westminster) was a popular choice because he had a fine singing voice and enjoyed entertaining the children with ballads. He was the inspiration for the Duck in the story.

'What I was going to say,' said the Dodo in an offended tone, 'was that the best thing to get us dry would be a Caucus-race.'

Dodgson shows his opinion of a caucus – a meeting to decide political party policy – by turning it into a pointless chaotic event with everyone running around in circles. The now extinct Dodo not

only represents him and the way
he sometimes stammered his name,
but was also chosen because every
Oxford child had been taken to see
John Savery's painting of a dodo in
the University Museum. Alice and
her sisters would almost certainly
have known the picture.

"'Twinkle, twinkle little bat!
How I wonder what you're at!"
'You know the song, perhaps?' [the
Hatter asks Alice].
'I've heard something like it,' said Alice.
"'Up above the world you fly,
Like a tea-tray in the sky.'" ...

Alice's father, the Dean, knew all
the professors, many of whom were
often seen at the Deanery. One
of these learned men, Professor
Bartholomew Price, a great friend

and former tutor of Dodgson's, was always known as 'Bat' because it was said, when he was lecturing, his words always flew over everybody's heads. This rhyme cunningly weaves him into the story.

In a minute or two the Caterpillar took the hookah out of its mouth and yawned once or twice, and shook itself. Then it got down off the mushroom, and crawled away into the grass, merely remarking as it went, 'One side will make you grow taller, and the other side will make you grow shorter.'

Alice nibbles a piece of mushroom and, to her consternation, finds she has grown *'an immense length of neck, which seemed to rise like a stalk …'*

In the fireplaces in Christ Church Hall, where the dons and Alice's father dined with the students, are decorative firedogs each with a long brass 'neck' topped with a woman's head. John Tenniel's illustration of Alice with her stalk-like neck seems to have been inspired by these firedogs.

'All right,' said the Cat; and this time it vanished quite slowly, beginning with the end of the tail, and ending with the grin, which remained some time after the rest of it had gone. 'Well! I've often seen a cat without a grin,' thought Alice; 'but a grin without a cat! It's the most curious thing I ever saw in all my life!'

It was from the window of Christ Church's library that Dodgson, appointed sub-librarian, first saw the three small Liddell sisters playing in the Deanery garden. Later he was often to spy Dinah, Alice's beloved cat, sitting in the branches of the chestnut tree that grew there. In the story Alice is clearly fond of Dinah, tactlessly mentioning her to the tetchy Mouse who tells her: *'Our family always hated cats: nasty, low, vulgar things!'*

Cheshire cats traditionally have fixed grins and it is thought Dodgson might have imagined this strange creature, who appears and disappears in parts, from seeing carvings of cat-like faces in his father's church in Yorkshire. He knew the idea of a friendly, grinning cat was bound to appeal to his young friend, the real Alice.

MEAN WHAT YOU SAY!

*'Then you should say what you mean,'
the March Hare went on.
'I do,' Alice hastily replied; 'at least –
at least I mean what I say – that's the
same thing you know.'
'Not the same thing a bit!' said the
Hatter. 'You might just as well say that
"I see what I eat" is the same thing as
"I eat what I see!"'*

Dodgson's love of wordplay and his
delight in playing word games with
his young friends shines through the
pages of *Wonderland* and *Through the
Looking-Glass*, as in this encounter
between Alice and the Hatter and his
friends gathered around the tea table.

The conversation ends when the Dormouse says, sleepily: *'You might just as well say that "I breathe when I sleep" is the same thing as "I sleep when I breathe"!'*
*'It **is** the same thing with you,'* said the Hatter …

Early in the story Alice had wept so much when she was lost and alone that a deep pool of tears had formed, into which she and 'a queer-looking party' of assorted birds and animals had fallen. The sodden creatures had swum to the shore and, shivering, debated how to get dry. The Mouse thought he had the answer: *'This is the driest thing I know,'* he said: *'William the Conqueror, whose cause was favoured by the Pope, was soon submitted to by the English, who wanted leaders, and*

*had been of late much accustomed to
usurpation and conquest ...'*

Dry though the Mouse's lecture
on English history was, it left the
company as wet as ever and it was
the Dodo, with his novel 'Caucus-
race', who eventually provided a
better solution.

Alice, aware that she had offended
the Mouse deeply by boasting about
the hunting skills of her cat Dinah,
tries to make amends once the race
is over:

*'You promised to tell me your history,
you know,' said Alice ...
'Mine is a long and sad tale,' said the
Mouse, turning to Alice, and sighing.
'It **is** a long tail, certainly,' said
Alice, looking down with wonder at
the Mouse's tail; 'but why do you call
it sad?'*

'*I dare say you never even spoke to Time!*' the Hatter remarks contemptuously to Alice when she dares to accuse him of wasting it. '*Perhaps not,*' *Alice cautiously replied:* '*but I know I have to beat time when I learn music.*' '*Ah! That accounts for it,*' *said the Hatter.* '*He won't stand beating ...*'

As Alice makes her way through Looking-Glass land, she enters a garden full of talking flowers:

'*How is it you can all talk so nicely?*' *Alice asks the Tiger-lily.* '*I've been in many gardens before, but none of the flowers could talk.*' '*Put your hand down, and feel the ground,*' *said the Tiger-lily.* '*Then you'll know why.*'

Alice did so. 'It's very hard,' she said, 'but I don't see what that has to do with it.'

'In most gardens,' the Tiger-lily said, 'they make the beds too soft – so that the flowers are always asleep.'

Alice has a long conversation with the lachrymose Mock Turtle, who tells her all about his schooldays under the waves – and the curious subjects he was taught: *'Reeling and Writhing, of course, to begin with … and then the different branches of Arithmetic – Ambition, Distraction, Uglification, and Derision.'*

Alice ponders uglification before asking what else he learnt.

'Well, there was Mystery,' the Mock Turtle replied, counting off the subjects on his flappers, '– Mystery, ancient and modern, with Seaography: then

*Drawling – the Drawling-master was
an old conger-eel, that used to come
once a week: he taught us Drawling,
Stretching and Fainting in Coils.'*

Alice learns about the classical
master, an old crab who taught
Laughing and Grief, before asking
how many hours a day the Mock
Turtle and his friend, the Gryphon,
studied:
*'Ten hours the first day,' said the Mock
Turtle: 'nine the next, and so on.'
'What a curious plan!' exclaimed Alice.
'That's the reason they're called
lessons,' the Gryphon remarked:
'because they lessen from day to day.'*

*'Where do you come from?' said
the Red Queen. 'And where are you
going? Look up, speak nicely and don't
twiddle your fingers all the time.'*

Alice attended to these directions, and explained, as well as she could, that she had lost her way.
*'I don't know what you mean by **your** way,' said the Queen: 'all the ways about here belong to **me** …'*

Humpty Dumpty is entertaining Alice:
'In winter when the fields are white, I sing this song for your delight – only I don't sing it,' he added, as an explanation.
'I see you don't,' said Alice.
*'If you can **see** whether I'm singing or not, you've sharper eyes than most,' Humpty Dumpty remarked severely.*

Alice, in the topsy-turvy land behind the Looking-Glass, remarks on the extraordinary gait of the King's two Messengers, Haigha and Hatta.

Peering down the road as Haigha approaches, she exclaims: *'What curious attitudes he goes into!' (For the Messenger kept skipping up and down, and wriggling like an eel, as he came along, with his great hands spread out like fans on each side.)*

The King tells her that, as they're Anglo-Saxon Messengers, they're striking 'Anglo-Saxon attitudes' – a phrase referring to a style of English drawing where the subjects are shown in swaying poses with palms held out in exaggerated positions. He then tells Alice that he must have two Messengers. She doesn't understand why, so tries, politely, to find out:

'I beg your pardon?' said Alice.
'It isn't respectable to beg,' said the King.

Many a conversation is thus led into a blind, if diverting, alley.

Alice feels the same frustration as she tries to be admitted to the house with her name, 'Queen Alice', in large letters over the arched doorway:

'Where's the servant whose business it is to answer the door?' she began angrily.
'Which door?' said the Frog.
Alice almost stamped with irritation at the slow drawl in which he spoke.
*'**This** door, of course!'*
The Frog looked at the door with his large dull eyes for a minute ... then he looked at Alice.
'To answer the door?' he said. 'What's it been asking of?'

CONVERSATIONS WITH CURIOUS CREATURES

'Curiouser and curiouser!' cried Alice,
having eaten a cake that made her
suddenly grow taller. But things
were to become even more curious.
From the grumpy hookah-smoking
Caterpillar and the sad Mock Turtle in
Wonderland, to the shopkeeping Sheep
in the land behind the Looking-Glass,
many strange creatures were to test her
patience and her sense of reality.

'What do you mean by that?' said the
Caterpillar sternly. 'Explain yourself!'
'I can't explain myself, I'm afraid, sir,' said
Alice, 'because I'm not myself, you see.'
'I don't see,' said the Caterpillar.

'I'm afraid I can't put it more clearly,'
Alice replied very politely, 'for I can't
understand it myself to begin with;
and being so many different sizes in a
day is very confusing.'
'It isn't,' said the Caterpillar.

Poor Alice, finding her size changing
constantly and her memory not
functioning properly, is hoping
for a friendly encounter, but the
Caterpillar is decidedly grumpy. *'I
wish the creatures wouldn't be so easily
offended!'* she thought.

However, he does hint that
nibbling at the mushroom might help
her grow to a decent size again.

'There's no sort of use in knocking,' said
the Footman … 'First, because I'm on
the same side of the door as you are;
secondly, because they're making such

a noise inside, no-one could possibly hear you.' …

'Please, then,' said Alice, 'how am I to get in?'

'There might be some sense in your knocking,' the Footman went on without attending to her, 'if we had the door between us. For instance, if you were inside, you might knock, and I could let you out, you know.'

Alice, outside the house of the Duchess, is arguing with the Frog-Footman who keeps telling her that he is going to sit outside the door *'on and off, for days and days'*.

'It's really dreadful,' she muttered to herself, 'the way all the creatures argue. It's enough to drive one crazy!'

'Who **are** you talking to?' said the King, coming up to Alice and looking at the Cat's head with great curiosity. 'It's a friend of mine – a Cheshire Cat,' said Alice: 'allow me to introduce it.' 'I don't like the look of it at all,' said the King: 'however it may kiss my hand if it likes.' 'I'd rather not,' the Cat remarked. 'Don't be impertinent,' said the King, 'and don't look at me like that!' He got behind Alice as he spoke. 'A cat may look at a king,' said Alice. 'I've read that in some book, but I don't remember where.'

'When we were little,' the Mock Turtle went on at last, more calmly, though still sobbing a little now and then, 'we went to school in the sea. The master was an old Turtle – we used to call him "Tortoise" –'

'Why did you call him Tortoise, if he wasn't one?' Alice asked.
'We called him Tortoise because he taught us,' said the Mock Turtle angrily: 'really you are very dull!'

Alice, chastised, waits for the Mock Turtle to continue:

'We had the best of educations – in fact, we went to school every day –'
'I've been to a day-school, too,' said Alice; 'you needn't be so proud as all that.'
'With extras?' asked the Mock Turtle a little anxiously.
'Yes,' said Alice, 'we learned French and music.'
'And washing?' said the Mock Turtle.
'Certainly not!' said Alice indignantly.
'Ah! then yours wasn't a really good

school,' said the Mock Turtle in a tone of great relief.

Alice learns a great deal more from the Mock Turtle who is evidently sad, sighing and sobbing. She pities him and asks his friend, the Gryphon: *'What is his sorrow?'*
'It's all his fancy, that: he hasn't got no sorrow, you know ...' she is told, although she does learn from the Mock Turtle himself that once he was a real Turtle.

'What is it that you want to buy?' the Sheep said at last, looking up for a moment from her knitting.
'I don't quite know yet,' Alice said very gently. 'I should like to look all round me first, if I might.'
'You may look in front of you, and on both sides, if you like,' said the Sheep:

*'but you can't look all round you –
unless you've got eyes in the back of
your head.'*

Alice tries to see what is on the
shelves in the dark little shop owned
by the knitting Sheep, but as fast as
she peers at one shelf, the goods all
flow on to another:

*'Are you a child or a teetotum?' the
Sheep said, as she took up another pair
of needles. 'You'll make me giddy soon,
if you go on turning round like that.'
She was now working with fourteen
pairs at once, and Alice couldn't help
looking at her with great astonishment.*

As Alice puzzles the scene changes:
*'Can you row?' the Sheep asked,
handing her a pair of knitting needles
as she spoke.*

'Yes, a little – but not on land – and not with needles –' Alice was beginning to say, when suddenly the needles turned into oars in her hands, and she found they were in a little boat, gliding along between banks ...

WE'RE ALL MAD HERE

After Alice tumbles down the rabbit-hole into Wonderland and, later, steps into the back-to-front world of life through the large Looking-Glass, nothing seems to make any sense. Alice is taken aback when, talking to her new friend the Cheshire Cat, she is told she must be mad:

*'In **that** direction,' the Cat said, waving its right paw round, 'lives a Hatter: and in **that** direction,' waving the other paw, 'lives a March Hare. Visit either you like: they're both mad.'*
'But I don't want to go among mad people,' Alice remarked.
'Oh, you can't help that,' said the Cat: 'we're all mad here. I'm mad. You're mad.'

'How do you know I'm mad?' said Alice.
'You must be,' said the Cat, 'or you wouldn't have come here.'
Alice didn't think that proved it at all; however she went on: 'And how do you know that you're mad?'
'To begin with,' said the Cat, 'a dog's not mad. You grant that?'
'I suppose so,' said Alice.
'Well then,' the Cat went on, 'you see, a dog growls when it's angry, and wags its tail when it's pleased. Now I growl when I'm pleased, and wag my tail when I'm angry. Therefore, I'm mad.'
'I call it purring, not growling,' said Alice.
'Call it what you like,' said the Cat.

Alice, who has already encountered the Duchess, with her pepper-shaking Cook and bawling baby that turns into a pig and runs off into the wood, might be considering the truth of the

Cheshire Cat's words. She walks on until she encounters a house with a large table set for tea occupied by the Hatter and the March Hare leaning on a sleepy Dormouse:

*'No room! No room!' they cried out when they saw Alice coming. 'There's **plenty** of room!' said Alice indignantly, and she sat down in a large arm-chair at one end of the table. 'Have some wine,' the March Hare said in an encouraging tone. Alice looked all round the table, but there was nothing on it but tea. 'I don't see any wine,' she remarked. 'There isn't any,' said the March Hare. 'Then it wasn't very civil of you to offer it,' said Alice angrily. 'It wasn't very civil of you to sit down without being invited,' said the March Hare …*

Poor Alice spends a confusing
teatime trying to deal politely
with the rather rude Hatter, to
understand the strange story of
the treacle well, told by the sleepy
Dormouse, and to work out exactly
how mad the March Hare is. As she
leaves the everlasting tea party she
looks back, to see the Hatter and
the Hare trying to stuff the poor
Dormouse into a teapot.

*'Are five nights warmer than one night,
then?' Alice ventured to ask.
'Five times as warm, of course.'
'But they should be five times as **cold**,
by the same rule –'
'Just so!' cried the Red Queen. 'Five
times as warm, and five times as cold –
just as I'm five times as rich as you are
and five times as clever!'*

Alice sighed and gave it up. 'It's exactly like a riddle with no answer!' she thought.

'Humpty Dumpty saw it too,' the White Queen went on in a low voice, more as if she were talking to herself. 'He came to the door with a corkscrew in his hand –'

'What did he want?' said the Red Queen.

*'He said he **would** come in,' the White Queen went on, 'because he was looking for a hippopotamus. Now, as it happened, there wasn't such a thing in the house that morning.'*

'Is there generally?' Alice asked in an astonished tone.

'Well, only on Thursdays,' said the Queen.

Alice, the proud owner of a golden crown, has perhaps the most exasperating and mad encounter of all with the Red and White Queens

in the peculiar back-to-front world
behind the Looking-Glass. She is
asked impossible questions (*'Divide
a loaf by a knife – what's the answer
to that?'*) and subjected to an
inquisition to discover if she really
was a Queen, as the crown suggests.

'Do I look very pale?' said Tweedledum,
*coming up to have his helmet tied
on. (He called it a helmet, though it
certainly looked more like a saucepan.)*
'Well – yes – a **little**,*'* Alice replied gently.
'I'm very brave generally,' he went on
*in a low voice: 'only today I happen to
have a headache.'*
'And I've got a toothache,' said
*Tweedledee, who had overheard the
remark. 'I'm far worse than you!'*
'Then you'd better not fight today,' said
*Alice, thinking it a good opportunity to
make peace.*

'We must have a bit of a fight, but I don't care about going on long,' said Tweedledum. 'What's the time now?'
Tweedledee looked at his watch, and said 'Half-past four.'
'Let's fight till six and then have dinner,' said Tweedledum.

As she works her way across the strange chessboard that is the land through the Looking-Glass, she meets many weird and seemingly mad creatures and characters, including the two fat little men, Tweedledum and Tweedledee. And the old nursery rhyme about the nice new rattle and the battle that followed falls from her lips:

'I know what you're thinking about,' said Tweedledum: 'but it isn't so, nohow.'

'Contrariwise,' continued Tweedledee,
'if it was so, it might be; and if it were
so, it would be; but as it isn't, it ain't.
That's logic.'

It seems as if the two tubby men
aren't going to do battle today, until
Tweedledum spots his nice new
rattle, dirty and broken, lying under
a tree – and the inevitable happens.

OF CABBAGES
AND KINGS

As Alice explores the 'Looking-glass House' behind the mirror on the wall in her own drawing room, she discovers a book on the table with strange writing. It takes her a while to realise it is a 'Looking-glass book'. So she holds it up to a mirror and reads:

'Twas brillig, and the slithy toves
Did gyre and gimble in the wabe;
All mimsy were the borogroves,
And the mome raths outgrabe.

The first and last verse of Dodgson's most famous poem, *Jabberwocky*, had been composed many years before he enlarged it for *Through the Looking-Glass*. The two volumes of *Alice* have become as famous for their nonsense-verse as for the weird and wonderful creatures and characters that people their pages.

The rather pompous Humpty Dumpty, who boasts that he makes words do a lot of work (and says he always pays the hard-working words extra), condescends to explain the difficult words in *Jabberwocky* for young Alice:

'"Brillig" means four o'clock in the afternoon – the time when you begin broiling things for dinner.'
'That'll do very well,' said Alice: 'and "slithy"?'
'Well, "slithy" means "lithe and slimy",' explains Humpty Dumpty, who says it is a 'portmanteau word'

with two meanings packed into it,
like 'mimsy' which means 'flimsy'
and 'miserable'.

She also discovers that 'toves' are
creatures something like badgers,
lizards and corkscrews, and that they
live under sundials and eat cheese.

'You are old, Father William,' the
young man said,
'And your hair has become very white;
'And yet you incessantly stand on your
head –
Do you think, at your age, it is right?'

When Alice encounters the
blue Caterpillar in Wonderland,
she confesses to him that she is
undergoing something of an identity
crisis, unable to control her height
and having difficulty remembering
things. The Caterpillar orders her to

declaim *You are old Father William*,
so she folds her hands and faithfully
repeats eight verses.

The grumpy Caterpillar is not
impressed. *'It is wrong from beginning
to end,'* he says.

Poor Alice is also scolded when she
tries to recite poetry to the Gryphon
and the sad Mock Turtle:

*'Stand up and repeat "'Tis the voice of
the sluggard,"'* said the Gryphon.
… the words came very queer indeed:
*"'Tis the voice of the Lobster; I heard
him declare,*
*"You have baked me too brown, I must
sugar my hair."*
*As a duck with its eyelids, so he with
his nose*
*Trims his belt and his buttons, and
turns out his toes.'*

Even the gentle Mock Turtle declares Alice's rendition *'uncommon nonsense'*.

But perhaps Alice could be forgiven, as, moments before, the unlikely pair had been excitedly explaining and demonstrating their favourite dance, the Lobster Quadrille, setting it to a strange song:

'Will you walk a little faster?' said a whiting to a snail.
'There's a porpoise close behind us, and he's treading on my tail.
See how eagerly the lobsters and the turtles all advance!
They are waiting on the shingle – will you come and join the dance?
Will you, won't you, will you, won't you, won't you join the dance?

'You can really have no notion how delightful it will be

When they take us up and throw us,
with the lobsters, out to sea!'
But the snail replied 'Too far, too far!'
and gave a look askance –
Said he thanked the whiting kindly,
but he would not join the dance.
Would not, could not, would not, could
not, would not join the dance.
Would not, could not, would not, could
not, could not join the dance.

'What matters it how far we go?' his
scaly friend replied.
'There is another shore, you know, upon
the other side.
The further off from England the
nearer is to France –
Then turn not pale, beloved snail, but
come and join the dance …'

Another song follows from the Mock
Turtle and, as Alice hurries away

with the Gryphon to the trial of the
Knave of Hearts, she hears the Mock
Turtle still singing:

Beautiful Soup, so rich and green,
Waiting in a hot tureen!
Who for such dainties would not stoop?
Soup of the evening, beautiful Soup!
Soup of the evening, beautiful Soup! …

Perhaps the favourite poem of all is
the one told by Tweedledum about
the Walrus and the Carpenter, and
their dastardly treatment of the
young Oysters who thought they
were being taken for a pleasant walk
along the seashore. It begins gently
enough:

The sun was shining on the sea,
Shining with all his might:
He did his very best to make

The billows smooth and bright –
And this was odd, because it was
The middle of the night …

Eventually we meet the villains of
the piece:

The Walrus and the Carpenter
Were walking close at hand;
They wept like anything to see
Such quantities of sand:
'If this were only cleared away,'
They said, 'it would be grand!'

They debate the possibility of *'seven*
maids with seven mops' managing to
clear the sand before the cunning
Walrus spots the oyster-bed:

'O Oysters come and walk with us!'
The Walrus did beseech.
'A pleasant walk, a pleasant talk,

Along the briny beach:
We cannot do with more than four,
To give a hand to each.'

The wise old Oyster declines the invitation but others were not so careful:

But four young Oysters hurried up,
All eager for the treat:
Their coats were brushed their faces
washed,
Their shoes were clean and neat –
And this was odd, because, you know,
They hadn't any feet.

Four other Oysters followed them,
And yet another four;
And thick and fast they came at last,
And more, and more, and more –
All hopping through the frothy waves,
And scrambling to the shore.

After a mile or so they stop for a rest:

'The time has come,' the Walrus said,
'To talk of many things:
Of shoes – and ships – and sealing wax –
Of cabbages – and kings –
And why the sea is boiling hot –
And whether pigs have wings.'

Then the tone changes. The fat
little Oysters confess to being out of
breath and the Walrus ponders:

'A loaf of bread,' the Walrus said,
'Is what we chiefly need:
Pepper and vinegar besides
Are very good indeed –
Now if you're ready, Oysters dear,
We can begin to feed.'

Alice listens to the poem all the
way through to the last verse, when

she decides that both the Walrus
and the Carpenter were unpleasant
characters:

'O Oysters,' said the Carpenter.
'You've had a pleasant run!
Shall we be trotting home again?'
But answer came there none –
And this was scarcely odd, because
They'd eaten every one.

OFF WITH
THEIR HEADS!

Alice, at just seven years old, is a
self-possessed small girl, who faces
not only the curious happenings
that confront her, but also the often
frightening situations and people,
with equanimity and a calmness that
belies her age.

Spying a White Rabbit with
pink eyes and wearing a waistcoat
scuttling past her is astonishing
enough, but when she sees him take
a watch out of his waistcoat pocket
and hears him muttering to himself
'Oh dear! Oh dear! I shall be too late!',
she follows him without thinking
what she is doing.

She *'was just in time to see it pop down a large rabbit-hole under the hedge. In another moment down went Alice after it, never once considering how in the world she was to get out again.'*

In just a few seconds she finds herself tumbling down and down what seems like a bottomless shaft:

'Well!' thought Alice to herself, 'after such a fall as this, I shall think nothing of tumbling down stairs! How brave they'll think me at home! Why I wouldn't say anything about it, even if I fell off the top of the house!'

If the long fall itself, into what Alice believes to be the centre of the earth, wasn't frightening enough, her next adventure is probably even more disturbing. In her desperation to get through a small door into *'the*

loveliest garden you ever saw' she
drinks potions and nibbles cakes,
which in turn make her grow tiny
and large. But frustration grows as
the key to the garden gate is out of
reach and Alice at last begins to sob,
crying so much that she finds herself
swimming in a pool of her own tears:

*'I wish I hadn't cried so much,' said
Alice, as she swum about, trying to find
her way out. 'I shall be punished for it
now, I suppose, by being drowned in my
own tears!'*

Another crisis occurs as Alice, inside
the White Rabbit's tidy little house,
stops to sip from another of those
mysterious little bottles. She grows
so large that she becomes firmly
wedged and hears the Rabbit and his
friends making plans to extricate her

by burning the house down. But she keeps her head, remembering how mention of her cat, Dinah, seems to frighten the small animals in Wonderland:

Alice called out as loud as she could, 'If you do, I'll set Dinah at you!'

This threat does the trick and, instead of the drastic action proposed, they bombard her with pebbles that turn into tiny cakes that, when eaten, shrink her to midget proportions.

After this Alice is hardly rattled when, arguing with the Frog-Footman outside the noisy house of the Duchess, she hears *'howling and sneezing, and every now and then a great crash, as if a dish or kettle had been broken to pieces.'*

Despite the disorderly noises, she slips in, uninvited, to the Duchess's kitchen, where a belligerent Cook is sprinkling pepper and stirring soup. A large grinning cat sits on the hearth, while the Duchess nurses a howling baby. As Alice racks her brains for a topic of conversation, things turn unpleasant:

… *the cook took the cauldron of soup off the fire, and at once set to work throwing everything within her reach at the Duchess and the baby – the fire-irons came first; then followed a shower of saucepans, plates and dishes. The Duchess took no notice of them even when they hit her; and the baby was howling so much already, that it was quite impossible to say whether the blows hurt it or not.*

*'Oh, **please** mind what you're doing!'*
cried Alice, jumping up and down in
an agony of terror. 'Oh, there goes his
***precious** nose,' as an unusually large*
saucepan flew close by it, and very
nearly carried it off.

The Duchess seems unconcerned
and begins a rough lullaby, shaking
the baby violently as she sings:

Speak roughly to your little boy
And beat him when he sneezes:
He only does it to annoy,
Because he knows it teases.

When the Duchess finishes, she
flings the baby at Alice who carries it
outside and is rather relieved when it
turns into a pig and trots off into the
wood, grunting to itself.

Perhaps the most frightening character of all is the Queen of Hearts, whose solution to any difficulty is to order a beheading.

Alice is pleased to be invited to play croquet, but finds the Queen's approach alarming:

All the time they were playing the Queen never left off quarrelling with the other players and shouting 'Off with his head!' or 'Off with her head!' Those whom she sentenced were taken into custody by the soldiers, who of course had to leave off being arches to do this, so that by the end of half an hour or so there were no arches left, and all the players, except the King, the Queen, and Alice, were in custody and under sentence of execution.

In the giant chessboard that is Looking-Glass land, the characters and creatures are, on the whole, less aggressive than those in Wonderland, although Alice has an uneasy moment when she first meets the Unicorn, who periodically meets the Lion to fight for the crown.

The Unicorn, fresh from an encounter with his old foe, happens to spot Alice as he saunters past *'with his hands in his pockets'*:

… he turned round instantly, and stood for some time looking at her with an air of the deepest disgust. 'What – is – this?' he said at last.

On being told 'this' is a 'child', he is astounded:

'I always thought they were fabulous monsters!' said the Unicorn. 'Is it alive?' ...

... Alice could not help her lips curling up into a smile as she began: 'Do you know, I always thought Unicorns were fabulous monsters, too! I never saw one alive before!'

'Well, now that we have seen each other,' said the Unicorn, 'if you believe in me, I'll believe in you. Is that a bargain?'

YOU'RE NOTHING
BUT A PACK OF CARDS!

Games, puzzles and riddles were
what delighted Dodgson and his
young friends. He was close enough
to Alice Liddell and her sisters to
know that they enjoyed playing cards
and chess and games of croquet.
They loved riddles too.

Wonderland, with its strange
creatures who ask often
unanswerable riddles, is ruled
by a Queen and King inspired
by the figures in a pack of cards.
The royal rulers of Looking-Glass
land are chess pieces, while the
country itself is based on a giant
chessboard.

The Hatter opened his eyes very wide … but all he said was, 'Why is a raven like a writing-desk?'
'Come, we shall have some fun now!' thought Alice. 'I'm glad they've begun asking riddles. – I believe I can guess that,' she added aloud.

But she is diverted by more confusing conversation before the Hatter asks: *'Have you guessed the riddle yet?'* …
'No, I give it up,' Alice replied: 'what's the answer?'
'I haven't the slightest idea,' said the Hatter.
'Nor I,' said the March Hare.

Alice's journeys through Wonderland and the world behind the Looking-Glass are beset by such frustrations that leave her puzzled and exasperated.

A large rose-tree stood near the entrance of the garden: the roses growing on it were white, but there were three gardeners at it, busily painting them red. Alice thought this a very curious thing, and she went nearer to watch them, and just as she came up to them, she heard one of them say, 'Look out now, Five! Don't go splashing paint over me like that!'

The gardeners begin to argue until, suddenly, one of them spots Alice who asks why they are painting the roses:

Two began in a low voice, 'Why the fact is, you see, Miss, this here ought to have been a red rose-tree, and we put a white one in by mistake; and if the Queen was to find out, we should all have our heads cut off, you know.'

As the Queen enters the garden, which is also a croquet-ground, Alice begins to notice the strange shape of the ten soldiers, carrying clubs. Like the gardeners, they are 'oblong and flat, with their hands and feet at the corners', as are the ten courtiers who are ornamented with diamonds. The ten royal children are decorated with hearts and Alice realises that the gardeners are denoted by spades and that, of course, they are all a pack of cards.

She manages to protect the unfortunate gardeners from the angry Queen of Hearts, whose reaction to anyone or anything that displeases her is to shout 'Off with their heads!'

'Can you play croquet?' the Queen shouts at Alice, who joins the strange party to discover a game unlike any she had played before:

The balls were live hedgehogs, the mallets live flamingos, and the soldiers had to double themselves up and to stand on their hands and feet to make the arches.

The chief difficulty Alice found at first was in managing her flamingo: she succeeded in getting its body tucked away, comfortably enough, under her arm, with its legs hanging down, but generally, just as she had got its neck nicely straightened out, and was going to give the hedgehog a blow with its head, it would twist itself round and look up at her face, with such a puzzled expression that she could not help burst out laughing: and when she had got its head down, and was going to begin again, it was very provoking to find that the hedgehog had unrolled itself and was in the act of crawling away ...

'I don't think they play at all fairly,'
she complains to her friend the
Cheshire Cat, who chooses to appear,
partially, during the game. But the
real Alice must have found this
chapter diverting, because two of her
passions – card games and croquet –
are central themes in the story.

'You're nothing but a pack of cards!'
she shouts in the courtroom during
the trial of the Knave of Hearts. Now
back to her normal size she argues
with the Queen who would like to
see her beheaded. Wonderland and
its characters dissolve and Alice
wakes up on a shady bank in her
garden, her head safely in the lap of
her older sister.

*For some minutes Alice stood without
speaking, looking out in all directions*

*over the country – and a most
curious country it was. There were a
number of tiny little brooks running
straight across it from side to side,
and the ground between was divided
up into squares by a number of little
green hedges, that reached from
brook to brook.*

'*I declare it's marked out just like a
large chessboard!*' Alice said at last.
'*There ought to be some men moving
about somewhere – and so there are!*'
*she added in a tone of delight, and
her heart began to beat quick with
excitement as she went on.* '*It's a great
huge game of chess that's being played
– all over the world – if this is the
world at all, you know. Oh, what fun
it is! How I wish I was one of them! I
wouldn't mind being a Pawn, if only I
might join – though of course I should
like to be a Queen best.*'

Both Alice's wishes are granted: the Red Queen nominates her to be the White Queen's Pawn and tells her if she manages to travel to the Eighth Square she will become a Queen.

And, after many adventures, she reaches the Eighth Square, with the help of the White Knight, who rescues her from the clutches of the Red Knight as he tries to take her prisoner. Alice tells her rescuer: '*I want to be a Queen.*'

'*So you will, when you've crossed the next brook,*' said the White Knight. '*I'll see you safe to the end of the wood – and then I must go back you know. That's the end of my move.*'

The White Knight, an unsteady rider who tumbles frequently from his patient horse, delivers her to the limits of the Seventh Square before he turns to go back. Alice stays to wave

him off before she bounds across the
brook into the Eighth Square:

'Oh, how glad I am to get here! And
what is this on my head?' she exclaimed
in a tone of dismay, as she put her
hands up to something very heavy, that
fitted tight all round her head.
'But how **can** it have got there without
my knowing it?' she said to herself, as
she lifted it off, and set it on her lap to
make out what it could possibly be.
It was a golden crown.